HOW TO DRAW! DRAWING LESSONS

Drawing for Kids

Children's Craft & Hobby Books

All Rights reserved. No part of this book may be reproduced or used in any way or form or by any means whether electronic or mechanical, this means that you cannot record or photocopy any material ideas or tips that are provided in this book.

Copyright 2016

Are you an aspiring artist?

This drawing workbook will help you practice your hand strokes and fine motor skills.

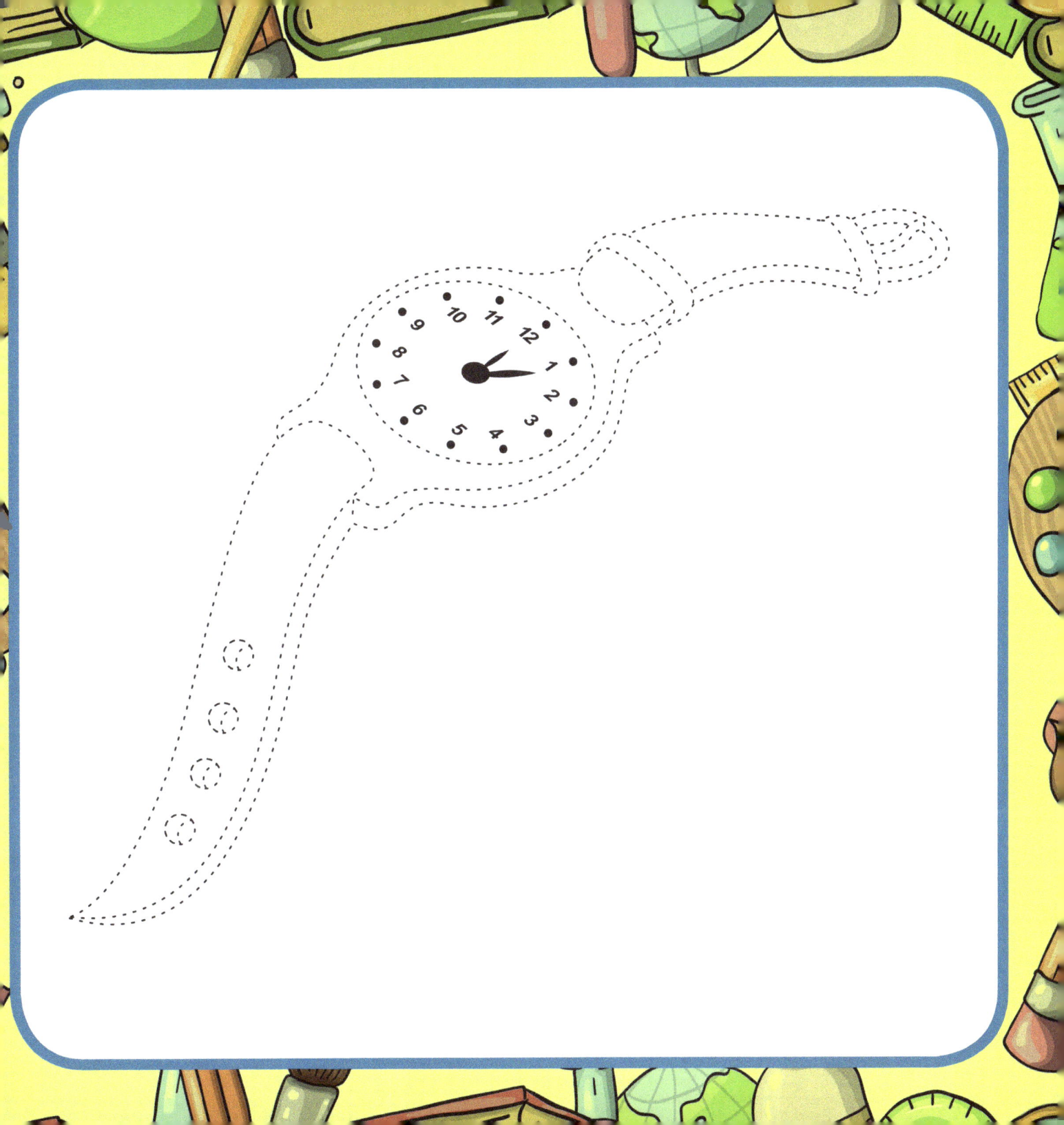

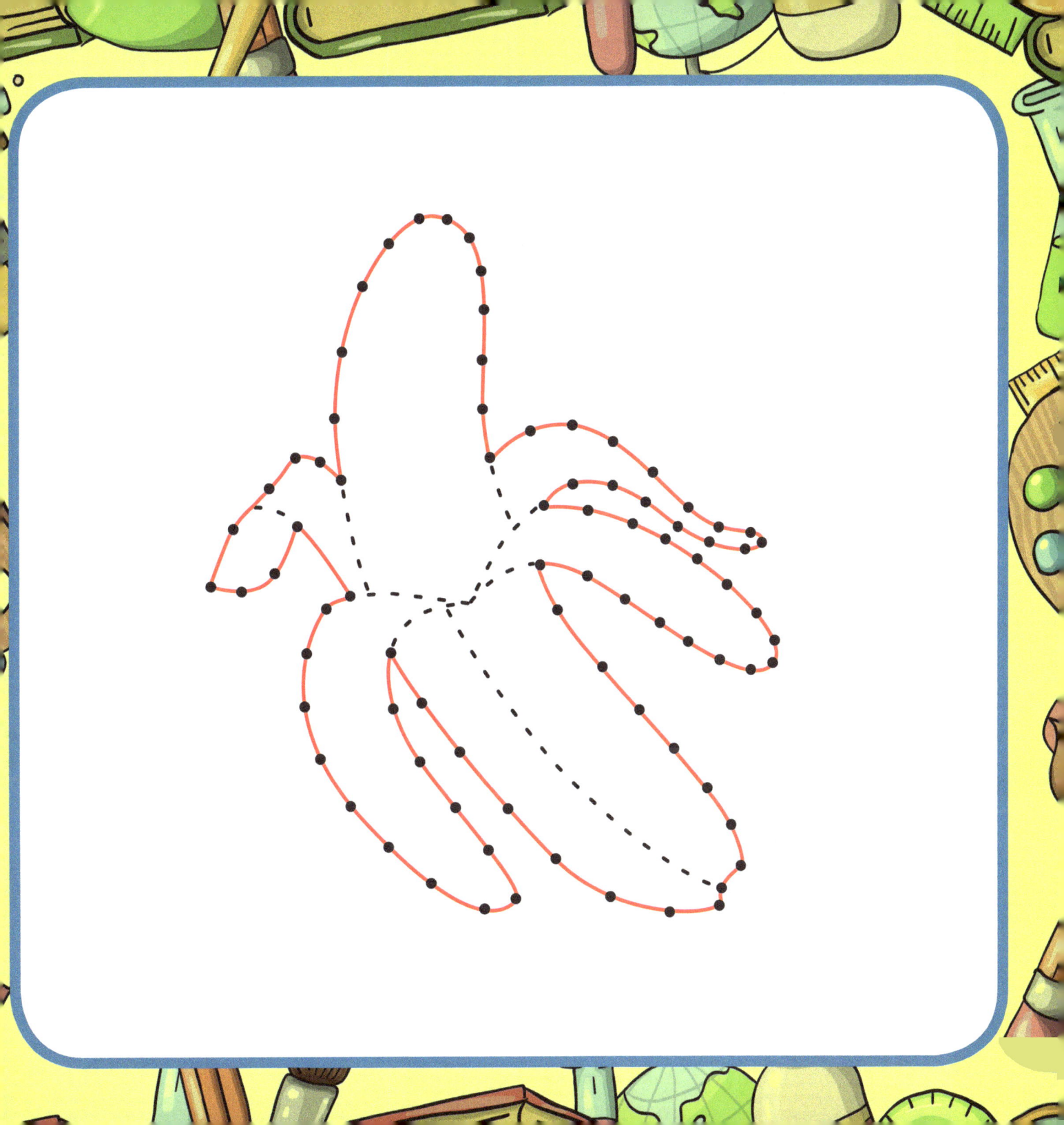

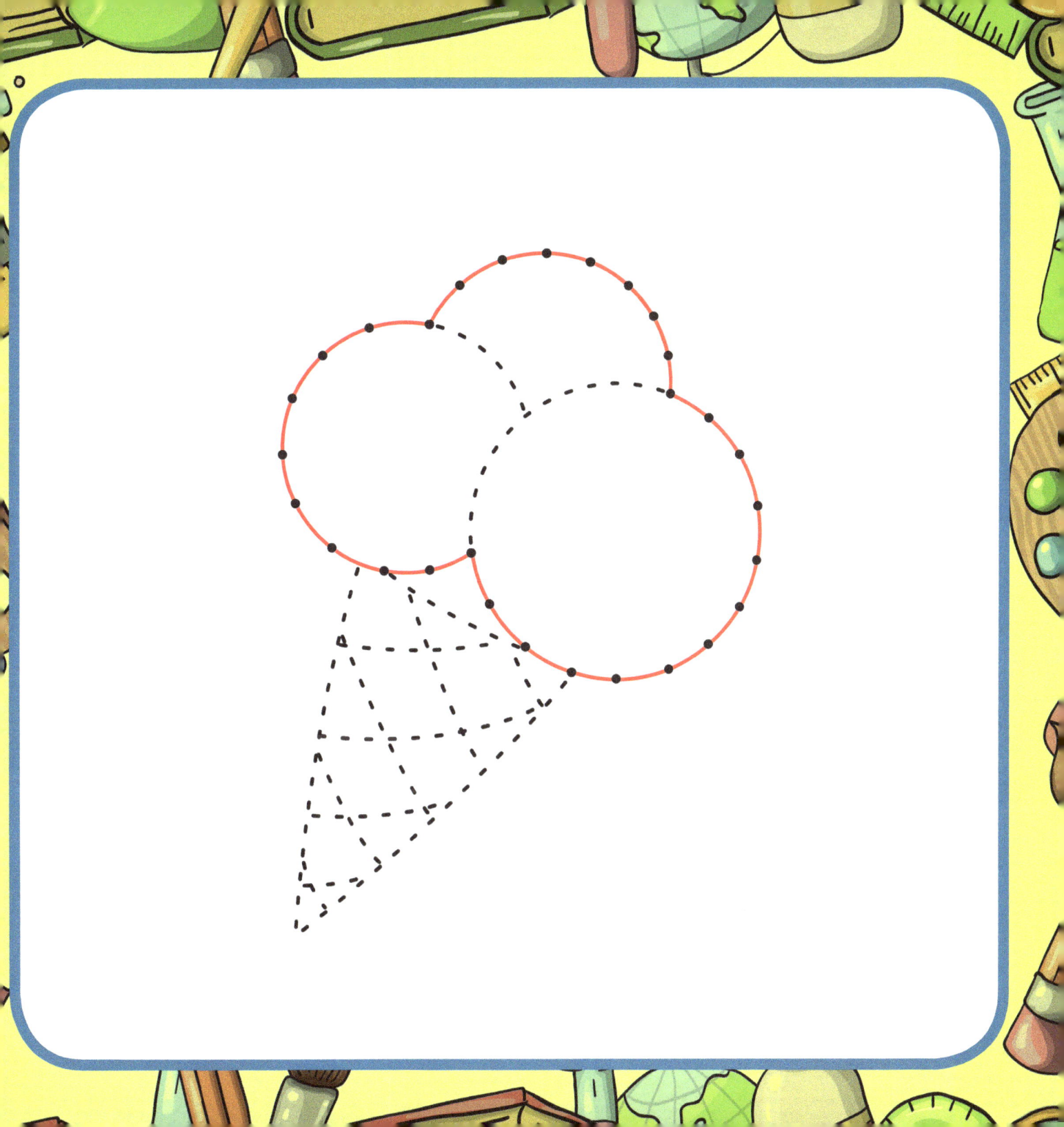

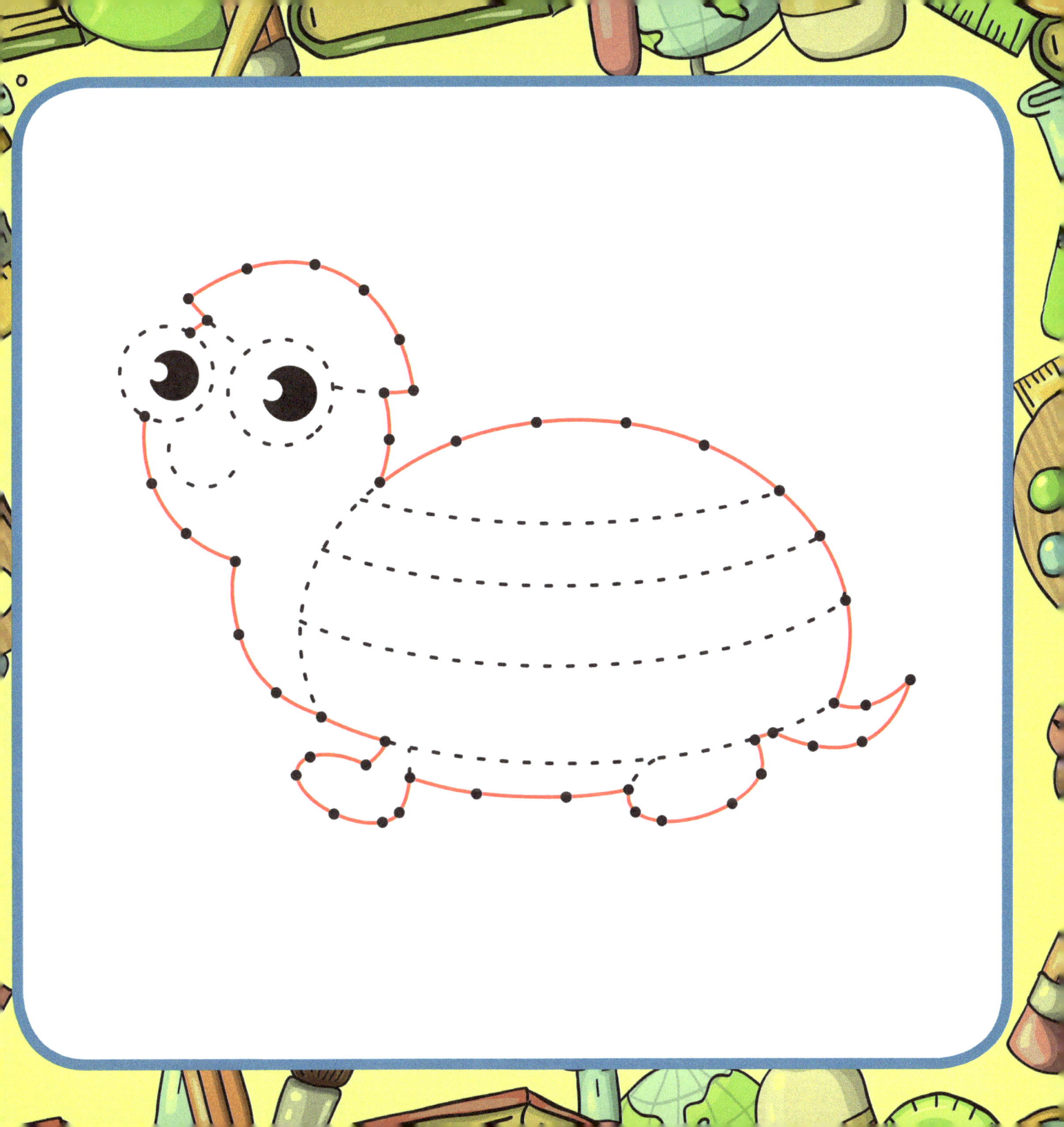

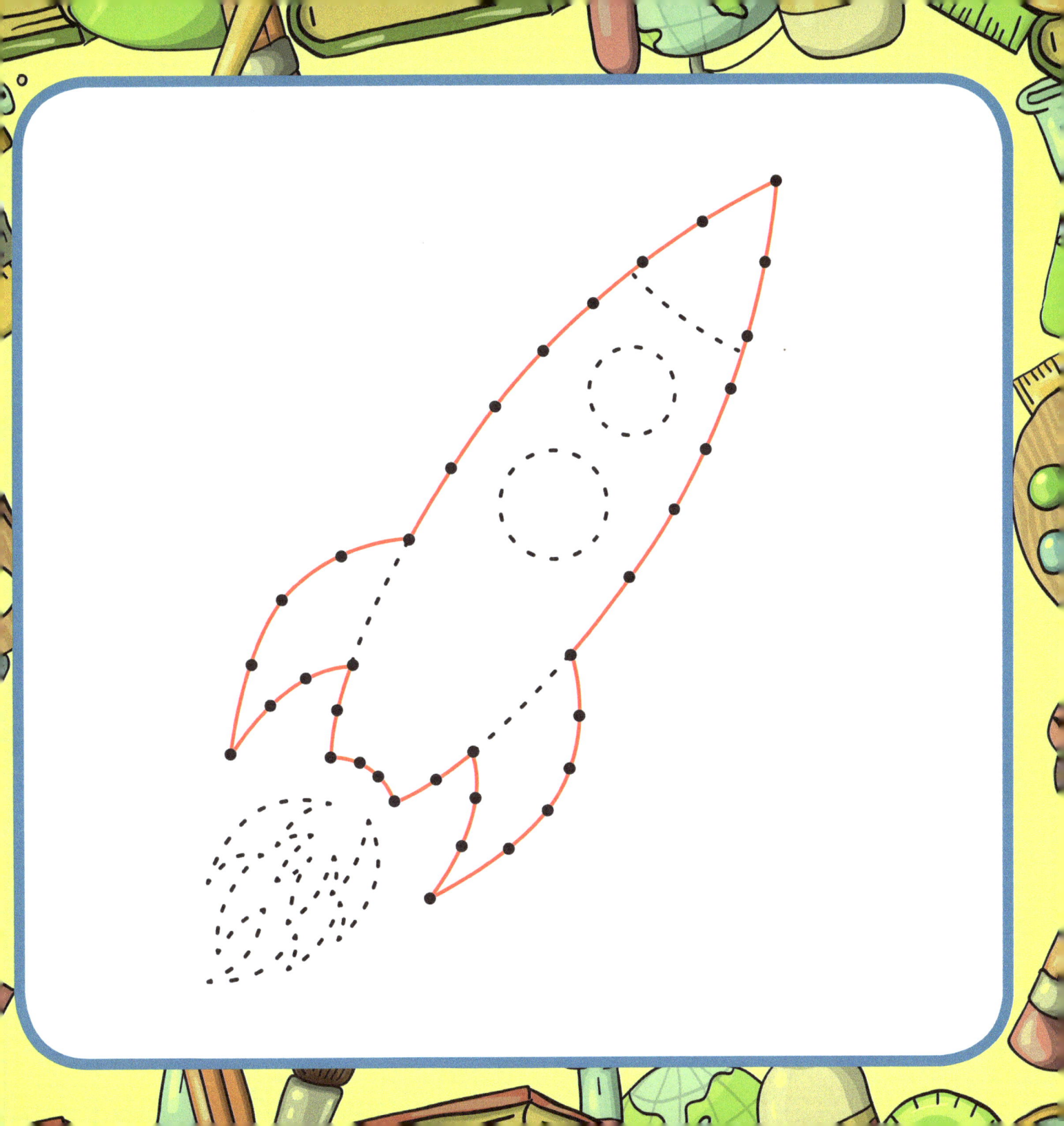

www.ingramcontent.com/pod-product-compliance
Lightning Source LLC
LaVergne TN
LVHW082253070426
835507LV00037B/2279